Get Your First Job as a University Student

10 Stories from University Students

Arthur Lee

Arthur Lee Books
Melbourne, Australia

Copyright © 2021 Arthur Lee

www.arthurlee.com.au

All rights reserved. No part of this book may be reproduced, or stored in a retrieval system, or transmitted in any form or by any means, electronic, mechanical, photocopying, recording, or otherwise, without express written permission of the publisher.

Every effort has been made to trace or contact all copyright holders. The publishers will be pleased to make good any omissions or rectify any mistakes brought to their attention at the earliest opportunity.

ISBN: 9798467906133
Imprint: Independently published

Arthur Lee
PO Box 161, Forest Hill VIC 3131
Australia
ABN: 29 172 617 138

Contents

From student to employer 1

Working to survive 5

Working for independence and experience 11

Developing confidence through the first job 17

From video games to mechatronics and tech 23

Growing into adulthood through work 29

Writing, trading and building business 35

Ask your friends and family when seeking a job 41

Freelance writer working towards neurosurgery 47

Being true to yourself 53

Dreams of working abroad 59

Afterword 63

Acknowledgements

From top left to bottom right: Abubakar Abdulsalam, Amr Ehab, Hasanat Noon, Hussain Samuaan, Jane Wanja, Lewis Mchardy, Noor Qaiser, Pamela Hellyer, Yigitcan Karagoz, Zenith Arbois

From student to employer

It has been an amazing journey as I reflect back on the life that I have had since the first day I started university in 1997. I was enrolled in a Bachelor of Physiotherapy, and I still remember lining up for my university ID photo, the clothes that I was wearing, and meeting someone new who was standing behind me in line. We ended up becoming friends and he eventually ended up being the best man at my wedding.

I had a job tutoring high school students. I actually saw it as less of a job because I had to manage the workload, payments and didn't have a boss. I was running a little business. My parents were very supportive and would give me what I asked for, but this little business gave me a bit of independence and allowed me to spend as I wanted.

After four years of studying, I managed to tutor roughly 20 students a week. I have a memory of showing my parents a big stack of cash that I had managed to save up over a few weeks. Eventually I stopped tutoring because I was heading on a different journey in terms of my life goals.

That was a long time ago. My more recent memories have been hiring people during their course of study; from part time high school students to people in their journey towards a masters in their field. I loved working with students in one of my first major businesses. They gave me insight into a new world, they brought energy, and they brought knowledge. I have always enjoyed giving a chance for people to have something that they can take further into their career.

As I read stories in this book, I have received a new insight into the minds of the people that I hired over the years for local work, and in the freelancing space. Some have gone on to become leaders, some are health professionals, others are married, some have children, and yet many, I have lost contact with.

Was it really a new insight though? Or are my memories simply resurfaced. Do all generations have the same hopes, dreams and struggles?

In this book I reflect on my own experiences and ask ten university students around the world five simple questions. Questions to get them and us to reflect on the views of a changing global society. Questions that I believe relevant to this generation and every generation.

Why did you choose your current university course?

What was your first job while you were studying?

How important is having a job for you while you are studying?

What are your hopes in life after graduation?

A word of wisdom for students trying to get their first job

I hope that you will be inspired by these stories. I hope that you can draw strength from the experience of these people. Maybe one day, you can share your story of success with those around you.

Get Your First Job as a University Student

Working to survive

Zenith Arbois - Philippines

Why did you choose your current university course?

I was born and raised in a lower class family in Cebu, Philippines. Ever since I started my education, as the eldest daughter in an Asian household, I was expected to do everything excellently. Even in preschool, I was expected to excel in my academics, and I did. I worked hard for my grades and made sure I made my parents proud and happy. They said the grades were for me to get scholarships in the future for my higher education.

Unfortunately, I got burnt out in the middle of high school. I was still an honor student, just not the top student. When I got to college, our situation got even harder. My father became unemployed and my mother was a stay-at-home mom so, basically, I couldn't afford to be in a private university that offered what I wanted to take up. There weren't any full scholarships that I could access, and we weren't able to pay for discounted tuition either.

In order for me to compromise in our situation, I took up an examination in a state university to become a state scholar. Thankfully, out of about a thousand applicants, I was lucky to be one out of the two hundred who passed. I was so happy to be able to go to college without paying a single penny. I took up psychology because it's a very flexible course and I have always been in awe of how amazing the human mind is. Though it may not have been my top choice, it was my best possible option as it's the only program that I had an interest in.

What was your first job while you were studying?

I got my first job when the pandemic kicked in. It was around August of 2020 and I was in my second year in college. It was a call center job. My very first job. The position I got was a chat support representative for an online service in the USA and Canada. Because it was my first job, I won't lie about how hard the application was for me.

Call center companies here in my area take months before they view your application. Due to the pandemic, the industry was one of the few industries that thrived here in the Philippines. The interview process was hard for me as well. I never had an interview before and I didn't know what to expect. I read articles on Google to help me prepare myself while waiting for a call, but everything is just overwhelming and I couldn't help but feel extremely anxious all the time.

I also have a severe case of social anxiety, and this made me think I would screw everything up. Back in college, I actually cried in front of class when I reported a presentation. I didn't know why I really cried. My presentation was ready and I definitely knew what I was going to present. All I know is that I was shaking, stuttering, having cold sweats and suddenly tears rolled down my face. This also happened on one of my over the phone interviews, which I of course failed.

I just kept trying and applied to companies nearby that were hiring, until I got better. I finally aced an interview, passed the assessments, and finally got my first job.

How important is having a job for you while you are studying?

It's important for me to have a job even though I'm still in college, because we're stuck in a pandemic and both my parents are old and unemployed. Without me earning, we couldn't have made it through and we'd starve in the middle of a lockdown. Most of my income was going on my family's needs.

It was a shocker for me to realize how much money a family of four needs in a month to have something to eat and pay the bills. Four thousand pesos is not enough for groceries, and that's only for fifteen days. Plus, there's the electricity bill and other things that we need to budget for. I have around three or four thousand pesos that I keep in my savings. I tried to save up for a laptop, but my savings just kept getting used up.

Also, I wasn't too disciplined regarding money and budgeting, and I tended to impulsively purchase things that I didn't really need. Everything was hard. I was making sure I showed up to work, submitting my modules and homework on time, whilst also wasting money on food and trips I would always tell myself that I "deserved".

What are your hopes in life after graduation?

After graduation, I am still planning what I would really love to pursue. Like before, I still would like to have a career in arts and design, but I don't think that is possible with the course I have today. Maybe if our situation becomes better, I'll study design and build the career that I really want. Otherwise, I'll just push through with what I have and proceed in my education to become a certified psychologist.

Realistically, I'm looking forward to getting a job in corporate, and being part of a company's human resources team. Or I could reapply to a call center since they're always hiring and try to save up for a business that I could run with my significant other. I am still figuring out my options while I study, and I am still weighing up what I want with what is possible. Unlike before, I've now had a taste of what reality is like.

Opportunities are difficult to find, saving needs strict discipline, and you can't just give up on something after figuring out it's not really for you. Time, money, and effort is very valuable in the real world. It's difficult to force ourselves to become something that we can't afford. So aim for something possible, and try to see if you can reach your previous goal from there.

A word of wisdom for students trying to get their first job

Getting your first job is difficult. You don't know what to expect and what's best to do. Just make sure to do your best and be honest with your employer and with yourself during interviews. Each one of us has unique strengths, so be confident and don't doubt yourself. If other people can do it, so can you. If you can't, then you must be better than those people in other fields.

There will always be failure and the possibility of your application being declined. This will give you an idea as to what you need to improve on, or you can look for other jobs that would suit you better. You just have to be honest towards your employer and more importantly with yourself. Find a job that you'll enjoy doing. That way, you'd be less nervous and more confident. This will also be your first step in creating a successful career for yourself.

Since you're getting a job for the first time, there will be many adjustments that you will need to adapt to, and let me tell you, it's not easy. Make sure to at least talk about it with someone you can find comfort in, and that's a 10/10 recommendation. If you're still in school, it will be really hard as well. There will be a lot of things you'll need to balance, and you'll lose a lot of sleep, but I can assure you that it will be okay.

Personally, when things get hard and when I feel exhausted, I think of the salary I'll be getting on my payday, and when I do receive it, I feel a lot better. It will be a constant battle in your mind, but do know that with your hard work, you can be in a much better place in the future.

Get Your First Job as a University Student

Working for independence and experience

Yigitcan Karagoz - Turkey

Why did you choose your current university course?

Back in high school, I wasn't sure about what to in the future. I failed most of my classes and most of the STEM teachers were demotivating because I couldn't get the logic behind their classes. However, I've always felt a strong desire for English. I grew up watching English shows and programs, and also found the culture heartfelt. Maybe because of this, my English started to improve over time.

The only thing that I could do was English, and it made me feel important. Therefore, I wanted to go deeper into it. As a result, I had decided to study the English language teaching education program in one of my country's state universities. During my college education, I continued working at the same place I worked at during my high school years.

My English teachers always encouraged me to study English. With the help of language departments, it would open up more opportunities due to globalization. So, the right choice for me was to learn as many languages as possible to become a citizen of the world. Therefore, I would feel more connected to all cultures rather than only mine, creating a better version of myself for my future career.

What was your first job while you were studying?

I started working when I was in second grade in high school. I wanted to earn my own money without asking for it from my parents. So, I applied for every job that I could online. .

One of them got approved, and I started working as a consultant in a private language school. Since I was shy and had some insecurities, I wasn't able to fully communicate with people. So, being a stand consultant was really challenging, but I now tell myself that I did the right thing; during these times, I overcame my anxiety, and improved my communication skills a lot.

With improved communication and the urge to learn other cultures and languages, I met people like me, so I had the opportunity to come into myself and be myself more. Because of this, I was able to create a teaching career path by interning in a private language school. Furthermore, my co-workers and I mutually supported one another in our teaching and socializing skills. So, I now want to spend my time improving my teaching talents to give others the same opportunity that I had.

How important is having a job for you while you are studying?

I managed to pay for my own food and my own expenses for education, so I wasn't really dependent on my family for money. Moreover, I bought my very first phone with three months' worth of savings.

In terms of improvement, all I can say is that without that job, I wouldn't be the person I am today. It helped me in many ways, but the best part is that it helped me make connections, which affected my next job. Also, I was able to have hobbies and join extra social activities with the people I love, such as taking violin classes and going to the theater with friends. This also paved the way for me to improve myself socially.

Lastly, earning my own money made me feel less attached to my family and parents. I was the one who decided what to do and how to spend the money. Yet, I also was able to support my family in terms of bills and other expenses. From time to time, it gave me the courage that I had needed to live on my own. So, during my college years, I didn't suffer from house-chore-related activities and money management.

Step by step, I think things will become better; if we put ourselves into our work, whether we have positive or negative outcomes, we can succeed in everything that we put our minds to since it's experiences that are vital for human beings.

What are your hopes in life after graduation?

After graduation, I want to have a master's degree in my field while I work in a school, and I'll try to find chances to become a lecturer in a college. Education is essential for me, and as a teacher, I think we must improve ourselves in all ways. I also would like to have a chance to go and study abroad.

Since I like exploring other cultures, I always want to go and see them in first person. Whether Asia or Europe, culture is essential for the society that it creates, and I want to learn as much as I can. I see myself as an "earthling", so diversity is critical. Each individual has the potential to become more.

Rather than studying English language teaching, I also started to research child development in one of Turkey's state universities. It helped me to understand the families behind the students and why learning how to bring up children is essential. So, I also have some ideas about a school, or maybe a kindergarten mixed with language teaching, to help bilingually educated children become individuals who will find their own path.

Meanwhile, during the process, they will be surrounded by art so that they can learn how to feel, and how emotions are sacred to be spiritually guided and protected. But most importantly, change is a good thing, and they should realize that we need to accept how things happen, rather than trying to stop them from happening.

A word of wisdom for students trying to get their first job

Just do it! I know it's kind of embarrassing, or maybe you feel insufficient, but believe me, you need this. You will gain experience, and most of the time, you will feel motivated. You will start to believe in yourself, and most importantly, you will have a chance to further your career.

After graduation, your connections will be most important for you to find a job that you like and to be able to work with people that you love. So, working while studying will provide you with the surroundings in which you can create that opportunity.

Sometimes, theoretical education is not enough to be able to work in a profession. We need experience. If you are lucky enough to have that experience, you will have fewer problems while overcoming the challenges that you might face. The good thing is you can make friends. Your friends can embrace you with kindness and be there for you when you need them most.

In conclusion, you will be motivated both mentally and academically. The positive and negative experiences that you have will make you feel fantastic and push you to go further in your life.

Get Your First Job as a University Student

Developing confidence through the first job

Hasanat Noon - Bangladesh

Why did you choose your current university course?

I'm Hasanat Noon, born and raised in Dhaka, the capital of Bangladesh. I'm in the first semester of my junior year studying electronic and communication engineering at a renowned university in our country. I chose this course because I'm a technophile with an inquisitive mind, which means I want to research subjects to find out as much as possible. Since we are living in an increasingly digitized world where technology has become the mainstay for the majority of modern businesses, the need for competent engineering professionals is acute.

Technology runs on electricity and like every aspect of modern life, every sector also needs a stable electronic system to function daily. Moreover, once I have mastered electronics, I will be able to work in a diverse range of sectors. For example, involving electronics with the computer means that I can delve into computer architecture, combining electronics with industrial automations resulting in robotics. Combining electronics and communication with the computer and IT will get me into the IoT (Internet of Things), cell phones and home automation systems.

In short, my love for technology and its versatility is the main reason why I chose this course.

What was your first job while you were studying?

The first job I had while studying was tutoring some high school students. I got that job while I was waiting for the university admission test to happen. My exam was postponed for an undefined amount of time due to the Covid -19 situation. The whole city was under lockdown. I didn't have anything to do and I badly wanted to utilize my free time and start looking for jobs where I could work from home.

I applied to some news agencies for the post of a proofreader but got no response. At that time, one of my friends called me to ask if I could tutor her cousin who is in the 10th grade. At first, I hesitated because I had never tutored someone before. Also, as an introvert, this type of work sounded like a nightmare. But my friend kept insisting because I helped her with her studies and I was a pretty good student myself, so she thought I could teach her well. It was really hard to make up my mind. At one point, I agreed to her proposal and went to her cousin's address. Her family warmly welcomed me and told me to start teaching her from that day. To be honest, the first few days were a bit awkward as I was super shy but with time, I became more and more comfortable. I used to prepare notes, sample questions for her and explain every single topic clearly.

One day she mentioned that two of her friends also wanted to join the study session because they saw the notes and liked them a lot. I eagerly agreed as the payment was good and group study is one of the best ways to learn. I started to like teaching as it meant that I had to understand every topic in-depth, which helped me a lot with my studies and sometimes felt like killing two birds with one stone!

How important is having a job for you while you are studying?

Having a part-time job while studying is immensely important as it helped me gain skills that a university or college could never teach me. Being shy and introverted, a part-time job helped me to come out of my shell and grow my confidence. As well as confidence, it provides me with an opportunity to learn how to interact with different personalities which is an essential skill for all types of work.

I became better at time management and learned how to balance energy between activities. Also, earning money on my own increased my self-esteem. When I started making money, I became more cautious about spending. With my first salary, I brought presents for my parents and my little brother. They were so proud of me and honestly, nothing felt better than that. From the following month, I started saving up my income for my higher education as advised by my parents.

What are your hopes in life after graduation?

I'm currently in the process of deciding what I want to do with my life after completing graduation. However, I really hope to pursue a postgraduate degree. To broaden my experience and cultural horizons, I want to receive that degree from abroad. I think a postgraduate degree helps an individual to gain technical knowledge and the right skills. By taking advantage of those skills, one can grow both personally and professionally.

By the end of post-graduation, an individual eventually develops a decent personality and is all set for the professional world outside. I'm studying hard to establish myself as a successful engineer. I love new and innovative technology. It would be great if I could work as a researcher for any tech giant company.

I would love a job where I can work freely, do research-based work, and get a handsome salary. I feel that if a person works just for the sake of money, then there's no point in working. Yes, money is important, but no person can enjoy the work if they're only working there for the sake of money.

A word of wisdom for students trying to get their first job

To any university student trying to get their first job, you're amazing for trying. Whatever block you are coming up against, whatever pain you are feeling --it will pass, I promise. Try to learn new skills as much as you can because they'll give you access to new and different chances.

Moreover, developing yourself is personal growth. Sometimes, you need to take risks, challenge yourself, and try harder at things. It will help you to discover your shortcomings so that you can become a better version of yourself. But risks don't have to be reckless. If you fail in any work, try to adopt some skills that are related to that work and it will give you an advantage.

Whatever you do, don't forget to prioritize your studies. Lastly, don't lose hope. Work will come sooner or later if you keep doing your best. You are going to be amazing!

Get Your First Job as a University Student

From video games to mechatronics and tech

Abubakar Abdulsalam - Nigeria

Why did you choose your current university course?

I am studying Mechatronics Engineering at the Federal University of Technology, Minna. I come from Nigeria, where studying is compulsory and not simple. I spent most of my time schooling in a town called Okene. I had all forms of education there, including home training, before moving out for university.

While in high school, I spent most of my time playing video games or admiring technology and its feats. I was always curious and wanted to know how everything worked and came about. Often when I tried to acquire this knowledge, I ended up in trouble or with issues, but it was fun learning about how the world works.

When I graduated from high school I wanted to grasp more about the world and gain a degree. Getting a job in Nigeria is rather difficult unless you have much to offer, or your area of expertise is narrow, rare, and needed. At the time, the course Mechatronics Engineering was at its early stages. It was a new course, it had all I wanted in a course, and it is currently needed everywhere, so I insisted on taking it.

Get Your First Job as a University Student

What was your first job while you were studying?

When I successfully got admitted into the university I needed money for various reasons, so I went in search of a job that could cover a few of my expenses while studying. I came across an online freelancing website. It was a site with good reviews and customers so I signed up as a writing freelancer, and my application was approved.

At first, I was so joyful since the process of applying was hectic and time consuming, but that wasn't a problem. The problem will later be the issue of getting hired and verified. Since I'm not a verified freelancer yet and don't have any past jobs or reviews on my profile, no client will want to risk putting their jobs in my hands.

After applying for more than 20 jobs, I finally got an offer from a client searching for a new freelancer. I accepted his offer. The project was based on a business niche, and I was to write a thousand words on a very tricky topic at a low price, but since I needed a job to prove to future clients that I was good, I accepted it.

I was to create unique non-plagiarized content with zero grammatical errors, and the content should be optimized for SEO, and I was to provide it in 3 days. So, I went online and researched the given topic and provided the requested content with its requirement met. I submitted and got paid.

Get Your First Job as a University Student

How important is having a job for you while you are studying?

In Nigeria, getting a job is crucial to one's life in moving forward because money is needed to continue with life's daily activities. In reality, money is not free anywhere. Getting a job in Nigeria as a student is a big win because not all expenses could be placed on our parents. We just need that extra income for some necessities that can only be carried out by us.

Since I was a student, I needed money severely to continue most of my school activities like purchasing books, transport, feeding, accommodation, and extra expenses that school threw my way. So, I had to get a job to meet all these criteria or suffer the consequences. Thanks to freelancing, I got a job. I spent most of my income on daily living expenses in school, for getting a handbook, doing a project, purchasing something crucial to my studies, and other necessities.

I also spend my income on keeping myself up to date and on leisurely things like buying video games, consoles, a new pc, phones, and having fun during my free time. I also save sometimes so that I can buy something fun or for an upcoming occasion or event.

What are your hopes in life after graduation?

My initial aim at the university was to learn what I was interested in and make income from it. I would also like to have a fun-filled life after getting a degree, and aim to work as a robotics engineer, or even own a company or a firm on robotics engineering. I am happy with my course because I may have the privilege of working in different areas and sectors. Since it is a hybrid course it gives me access to several areas that are very interesting and overwhelming.

My main aim after graduation will be to get a job, but not just any job. Jobs I will be interested in will be robotics engineering, automobile engineering, or a consultant. I would not like to live a boring worker's life like working for the government or for minimum wage or less. After graduating and getting a degree, I plan to further my studies and get a certificate.

I also hope to impress everyone who ever supported me, like my family and friends. I would love to be as successful as one of our current global leaders in tech. I love his inventions and aims and would love to be more than him in the future.

A word of wisdom for students trying to get their first job

My advice for other students aiming to get their first job is to never give up; keep trying, keep learning and keep on getting better. Then, when it is your chance, you will soar higher than the eagle. For students on online freelancing sites, I advise you to not waste your time finding big jobs. Instead, spend most of your time getting your profile up and running, seek advice from different freelancers, and do not aim too high when job-hunting. While applying for projects, be sure to provide top-notch proposals or reasons why you are the best man for the job. Take it easy at first, learn how it is done, and make your own way of getting it done.

Your first job will matter a lot. It will give your insight into how good you are and will be your stepping stone to getting the next one. I think you should spend a lot of time crafting your profile because most clients do not just take proposals. They also survey profiles, and if your profile is top-notch, well-detailed, and crafted responsibly, then getting hired will be easy and smooth.

Also, make sure you do not leave any part of your profile hanging. If you have worked outside of the freelancing site, demand a testimonial from your client, and showcase it on the website or your workspace. My main advice is to always have patience, make corrections, and always try again.

Growing into adulthood through work

Pamela Hellyer - South Africa

Why did you choose your current university course?

My name is Pamela Hellyer and I have lived in beautiful South Africa all my life. I graduated from a small high school in 2019 with an eager and excited spirit to tackle adulthood! It's not that I didn't love high school, I genuinely enjoyed learning something every day, but at the age of eighteen, I wanted to gain experience in addition to learning.

I am currently a first-year university student at a long-distance learning university, the University of South Africa (UNISA). I chose long-distance learning as I live in a small town far from any mainstream universities and I'm not willing to give up my peaceful life for the city just yet!

I am doing my Bachelor's in Education in the Mathematics and Science stream. I chose this course because since I could remember, I have always been absolutely in awe of science. When I was thirteen years old, I did a school presentation on being an Astrophysicist... I really love science! However, I wasn't sure if I could manage as a scientist, being cooped up doing research. I needed a job where I could tell people about the world we live in and that is when I realized, at sixteen, that I needed to be a teacher.

My current course is four years long (or should I say four years short because time flies when you're having fun) and it's a combination of Science and Mathematics theory as well as Education theory.

What was your first job while you were studying?

I decided to take a gap year before studying in 2020. I wanted to get some hands-on experience in the working world before jumping back into books and examinations. I applied for many jobs, but it's not easy to get a job when you are fresh out of high school with no experience.

After a couple of weeks of sending my CV out, I got an interview and my very first job! Let me tell you this, there are very few things as gratifying as landing your first job because it is something that you alone, fought for.

My first job was as a personal assistant for two different companies at the same time and both were in the financial sector. What I learned at those jobs was priceless; responsibility and accountability, two things every student need as they enter their tertiary studies.

I resigned so I that could study full-time, as my job was far too demanding to be able to study and work at the same time. My dream was science and teaching - that was the path I knew I had to pursue.

So as of 2021, I became an official student, but I still needed an income. So, I applied for a few jobs but due to the pandemic, jobs were scarce. Fortunately, I landed a job at a clothing company as a shop assistant. I got this job through a recommendation from my sister-in-law who was resigning from her job at that same store. The position was part-time which was fantastic because studying was proving to be time consuming. It was the perfect job for a student as it was easy and quite relaxed compared to my first job.

However, I came to hear about an online platform where I could do content and creative writing which has always been a fun hobby for me. The income possibilities trumped that of a shop assistant. I have been a freelancer on this platform since.

How important is having a job for you while you are studying?

Although I still live at home with my mom and I am not compelled to pay rent, it's important to have an income of some sort. I am an adult and it's my responsibility to contribute to the household I live in. It's important to understand that from an early age, regardless of your family's financial status. It makes me feel more confident knowing that I am not a financial burden to anyone. I got a bursary for my tuition which only means I must work harder since I must reach a certain academic standard in order to keep studying.

I like to ensure that I don't keep my income for just myself, but that I also pay for some household necessities. Even if it isn't much, it's the principle that counts more. Also, having my own income means that I don't need to rely on anyone when there is something I need.

Having an extra income means you can spend money on recreation and getting together with friends and have guilt-free fun because it's your own money you're spending. However, this should be done modestly and with a budget in mind.

The skill of budgeting is a necessary one. While you live at home, practice structuring a budget, even if it's small. The point of a budget is to set priorities of where your funds need to go so that they aren't misused. My income as a freelancer is inconsistent, but I set percentages of where I want my money to go and I feel better knowing that I followed through with it. This is responsible and knowing that I am not abusing my hard-earned money gives me peace of mind.

What are your hopes in life after graduation?

After I graduate in 2024 (if all goes according to plan), I look forward to accepting a post as a high school science teacher. I am not too concerned about the type of school I work at, as long as I am fulfilling my role as an educator and mentor. From an experience I had while completing a teaching practical, I can honestly say that it is a morally rewarding job. It's not a high-paying career but I know that money can't buy the same joy one feels when making a difference in someone's life, even if it is just one pupil.

I plan to continue my studies while being a teacher, in the hopes of one day moving on to being a Professor for Astrophysics. That is a goal for the distant future, but I am relieved that my current university course aids that long-term goal. However, I am not in a rush to achieve this. I plan to enjoy as many years being a high school teacher as I can. I never want to take on more than I can handle. I prefer a calm and peaceful life to one where I am always cutting it short for deadlines.

A word of wisdom for students trying to get their first job

I haven't got many years of experience being a working student but in my one year of being a working adult, and my one year of being a working student, I have learned more than in twelve years of school. The real world is really where you take shape as an individual and it's important that you don't rush this process.

If you really want a job and you don't have the experience for it, bring ample amounts of energy and enthusiasm to your CV and your interview. Always be willing to learn. In that way, prospective employers will be more eager to teach you. Remember, most employers were university students once too so they probably know what you're going through. You will be surprised; some employers prefer that you have minimal experience. This means that they can mold you from a clean start.

Always be honest in your interviews and never lie about your university workload. You don't want to be in a situation where you must decide whether to miss a company deadline or a university deadline. Pick your battles. Be open from the beginning and ensure that your employer knows your priorities. While it is important to earn an income, it is also important to complete your tertiary course. After all, that is, what you set out to do when you registered as a student and made that commitment.

Don't be despondent if you've been on a few interviews and you still haven't gotten a job. Your interviewers might say that you're not right for the job, but then you must ask yourself, was the job really right for you?

Writing, trading and building business

Lewis Mchardy – United Kingdom

Why did you choose your current university course?

Throughout school, I was always changing what I wanted to do as a career. From Forensic Science to Law, nothing was off-limits. I was pretty good at the majority of subjects, but I really couldn't work out what I loved. When A-levels struck, I had to choose subjects. I chose Maths, Physics, and Chemistry because I enjoyed them; I was good at them and believed it would cover the most avenues for my ever-changing mind. As you can guess, choosing a university course became quite worrying. Most people say they have always known what they wanted to do, but I just can't believe that to be true.

While searching endlessly for the ideal degree for me, I finally found one that I could see myself doing, one that I would enjoy - a degree in chemical engineering. This fits me completely. It had the perfect blend of maths, design, and writing that I loved, without having to give up any of my passions. It is a degree sought after by many industries, especially ones I was considering going into, like petroleum engineering, finance, and investment banking. This is due to the skills you can develop on the course, like thinking under pressure and improving your eye for detail. I love the opportunities my course gives me, without making me feel pressured to stick to the same job my entire life!

After a lot of research, I decided to study at the University of Nottingham. This was a campus-based university, my preference, as well as being quite highly ranked for the degree I am studying. It also wasn't too far from home, which was a bonus as I could take my washing back every weekend!

What was your first job while you were studying?

My first two jobs as a freelance writer came at similar times. Both were copywriting jobs but were relatively unique in how I was writing and who for. This allowed me to develop my writing skills and give me the experience to start other jobs. The first of the two jobs were writing pages for a cryptocurrency play-to-earn website. I found the job and applied via an online freelancing site with a proposal, and after completion was asked to return when they had more work. This is a common occurrence if you are quick, hand in quality work, and have top communication. Clients do not like being left in the dark.

The second job is a long-term job, writing weekly blog posts for a fitness company. This is a ghost-writing project and provides me with experience in the copywriting style I want to pursue, allowing me to develop my writing in a tone that can resonate with the reader.

The difficulty in getting these jobs as an online freelancer mainly came from determining my niche. At first, I was trying to write everything. I applied to all types of jobs and my proposal was nothing but boring. However, I developed it. I reduced what I wanted to write about to industries I was interested in and somewhat knowledgeable in. I changed my proposals to something that was unique to the job and showed them what I can do. This has not only increased the number of job offers I get from proposals, but also gave me the opportunity to choose writing jobs I knew I would enjoy.

How important is having a job for you while you are studying?

The main reason I love to have my own freelance writing business while studying is that it allows me to escape my studies when things get tough and concentrate on writing. I can research and write about my passions all from my laptop and make an extra income with it. This extra income is especially useful for relieving the stress of having bills to pay, as I will always have this writing skill to be able to fund myself. This is why being a freelancer is so useful. Work whenever, wherever.

At the moment, a lot of the extra income I am making is being used in preparation for my graduation from university. I have a big interest in investing and trading, so I always make sure to put a little bit into my portfolios. I am also looking to build my capital so that I can invest in real estate, such as rental housing.

Some of my extra income does get used for fun! I love to travel, and as I start improving my business, I have the desire to travel the world! I have booked to travel to New York when I finish my second year of university and I am aiming to book even more as my freelance writing skills increase!

What are your hopes after graduation?

After graduation, my main aim is to grow my freelance writing business as well as become a full-time currency trader in the FOREX market. They have both developed into passions of mine and the ability to do them as a job would be amazing. I am hoping to start marketing myself and what I can offer to businesses directly, rather than staying on freelancing sites as I feel this is what can make you renowned as a freelancer. Linking with people and businesses on social networks can definitely help get your name out there, alongside your business!

I dream about being able to travel the world, and working remotely from my laptop would allow me to do this. The main goal in life is to have the ability to do what you enjoy and stay happy, which is why advancing myself as a freelancer and trader at university is so important. It gives me that head start in life.

I would also love to start my own blog and a video channel, documenting my travels. More specifically, the food I eat while traveling. I can only imagine what an amazing job trying food challenges all over the world would be!

A word of wisdom for students trying to get their first job

My first and foremost word of wisdom to people trying to get their first freelance job is to stop researching it and get started. Stop staring at articles about being a freelancer and start taking action. To get freelance jobs you need to apply for them. People are not going to come to you straight away. Tell your friends and family and ask them if they know anyone looking for a freelancer in your niche. If you don't have a niche yet, find it by applying to jobs!

My second word of wisdom is to treat your freelancing as an actual business, not just a hobby on the side. Market yourself, make a website, have your own business name. Not only will this come across as more professional, but it will also put you in the right mindset when marketing yourself to clients and for jobs.

My third and final word of wisdom is to make sure your proposal is actually going to resonate and be remembered by the client. They probably get hundreds of proposals a day, and your generic proposal you send to everyone else is going to be chucked to the side. Determine what they are looking for, write a catchy intro, and show them what you can do!

Get Your First Job as a University Student

Ask your friends and family when seeking a job

Noor Qaiser - Pakistan

Why did you choose your current university course?

Unlike most of my friends who spent their childhood years playing freeze tag and climbing trees, I stayed indoors, reading and daydreaming. I was raised in a middle class, Catholic family and attended a well-reputed school run by nuns, who were keen on molding us into virtuous young women.

I studied subjects of biological sciences in school and dreamt of having a career in healthcare services ever since I was a child. I followed my heart and went to college to study Food Science and Human Nutrition. A couple of close friends and a teacher of mine also suggested that I study this as my major.

The majority of the women in Pakistan lack knowledge about a nutritious diet and have poor pregnancy outcomes. The infants born either die at an early age or suffer from chronic illnesses such as cardiovascular diseases, diabetes, obesity, osteoporosis and cancer, later in life. Most of the deaths in Pakistan are caused by chronic diseases and I believe that I can make a difference by educating as many people as I can, especially the women.

That is the reason I want to study Food and Nutrition in college so that I can help people in living a healthy lifestyle.

What was your first job while you were studying?

My first job as a student was teaching spoken English to kindergarten children via video conferencing. My father was facing a financial crisis and he wanted me to find work so that I could pay for college myself. He talked to his friend whose niece happened to be the director of my college and was looking for someone who could teach her daughter and nephews spoken English.

My father's friend suggested she hire me, and she agreed when she heard that I was a past pupil from Convent, a British school that was very strict when it came to grammar and pronunciation. Living among the pandemic, she wanted me to teach them through video calls.

We started the very next day, and it was very hard for me as I had no experience dealing with children, leave alone teaching them online. They could not sit still in front of a screen and answering their weird questions seemed impossible to me.

There was a day when a six-year-old boy sat in front of the screen crying with frustration, while his eight-year-old brother was looking at him and laughing that evil laugh. I was simply clueless and had no idea whether to sympathize with the boy or to laugh at his brother's expressions. I ended up showing them a cartoon to divert their attention. It was hard during the first week but as time went on, I started to understand their mindsets and bond with them.

How important is having a job for you while you are studying?

Having a full-time job while studying is not my thing as it puts you under a lot of pressure and can drift your focus from studying. However, you can always go for a part time job which I believe can give you a head start in your career. You will gradually learn to become independent, and you will get to know how to deal with people you work for and work with. You will learn to make connections just like I learned to connect with children.

Moreover, you'll be earning money to pay not only for college, but you can spend it on yourself too. With the leftover money, I buy myself the dresses that I have pictures of saved in my phone's gallery. This gives you one less trouble of having to go to your parents and convince them to buy you that.

Now, I can order food with my own earnings and satisfy my night cravings instead of waking my mother up and asking her for money. I can go out with my friends for lunch whenever I want to instead of eating cold food from the university's cafeteria. Life has been a bit better ever since I started working.

What are your hopes in life after graduation? What job would you like to get?

After graduation I plan on becoming a clinical nutritionist for which I need to earn the Certified Nutrition Specialty (CNS) which necessitates an examination and a thousand hours of practice experience. After I have completed my certification, I would be able to start my career.

As a clinical nutritionist I can opt for private practice or work in a hospital setting, whether inpatient or outpatient. I can counsel individuals and provide meal plans to those who are suffering from chronic diseases. Furthermore, clinical nutrition has a very competitive salary.

I also plan on taking the Central Superior Service (CSS) exams which are held by the Federal Public Service Commission of Pakistan. This is basically an entrance test to get a reputable government job with a very high salary. I can work as a food inspector or get a job in The Punjab Food Authority, an agency of the Provincial Government of Punjab in Pakistan, which makes sure of food safety and hygiene in the province of Punjab.

Having these high salary jobs would mean that I can go on vacations and have the keys to a luxury home and a luxurious lifestyle, which I've always dreamt of.

A word of wisdom for university students trying to get their first job.

Always ask your friends and family members first when you are looking for a job as they may know of an employer who is looking for someone who has just the right skills as you. You'll also feel more comfortable working for a person whom your well-wisher has recommended to you. Your friends and family are there for you and they would be happy to help you out. Having a personal connection with your hirer would also mean getting a little leniency.

Secondly, always be patient and don't give up. The first days are surely hectic but as time goes on, I assure you your job will start to look better. Unless something is awfully wrong or if you have found a better job do not give up.

With no job at hand, searching for one could become a wearisome task. First, take a look at your financial health status and if you feel that life will get hard without an income, do not give up. Keep working unless you find a better job. Always stay positive and try to find the good in your job and the people you work for and work with, or you will never be able to find a job that you are satisfied with.

Get Your First Job as a University Student

Freelance writer working towards neurosurgery

Hussain Samuaan - Malaysia

Why did you choose your current university course?

I'm a 21-year-old Maldivian currently studying MBBS (Bachelor of Medicine and Surgery) in the International Medical University of Malaysia.

I chose to study medicine for a couple of reasons. Firstly, I am always looking for a challenge and this is one of the fields that can really challenge me. Becoming a doctor is a long and stressful journey where there will be lots of ups and downs. Some people take those difficulties or obstacles as a setback in their path towards success. I, however, wanted to learn from those difficulties to become a better person.

Secondly, with the rapid development of technology, the healthcare industry is advancing faster than ever. Every year we learn something new about a disease or we find a new drug that could cure even the deadliest disease. So, I wanted to choose a field where I must continuously update myself even after graduation.

In addition, I love talking and caring for other people. I remember a time when I was 16, I witnessed someone choking at a restaurant. I had seen from the

TV what to do in such situations but when the opportunity came, I panicked and didn't know what to do. Then I realized that I needed more than just knowledge! In other words, I had to learn how to apply my knowledge in real-life situations. So, I promised myself that I would become a healthcare professional in the future.

What was your first job while you were studying?

I started to explore various ways I could get extra income. I found out that the best option for me was to freelance as I could be flexible and choose when and what type of work to do. That way, I could make sure my studies were not affected due to the high workload.

I joined a freelancing website and the main service I wanted to offer was medical content writing. However, no one was willing to hire me initially due to my lack of experience as a writer (of course I write every day for academic purposes, but clients want more than that). I spent a lot of time applying to writing jobs but with no success. I was really demotivated and thought that maybe freelancing is not for me.

But I refused to give up! I knew that freelancing would be hard and that if it was easy, everyone would be doing it. So, I kept believing in myself and decided to apply to jobs that were not exactly medical. What I mean is that I started applying to any job that matched my skills.

After weeks of trying, one day I finally received an offer for my first job. I was over the moon and wanted to do my very best. The job didn't pay much, but I didn't care. I just wanted to gain experience and show my knowledge and expertise to the client.

The job required me to be a participant of a science-based body type survey. It wasn't an ordinary survey though, there were lots of details and instructions to follow and I had to read each and every word carefully as it was important. I spent around an hour reading the instructions and another 2 hours to answer the questions. After answering the questions, I had to write a few comments regarding how the survey went and how it can be improved.

I submitted my work, and the client was really satisfied and gave me great feedback. Although it wasn't my dream first job, I loved it. Plus, the feedback I got helped me to land more amazing jobs later.

How important is having a job for you while you are studying?

I started my university course in 2020. I worked very hard during my A levels and was lucky to win a scholarship for my higher studies. The scholarship department takes care of my university fee and living expenses. However, due to my lifestyle, it is difficult for me to manage with the amount of money covered by it.

I am the kind of person who loves to go out and have a fun time with friends during weekends. I love to travel and whenever I get a holiday, I travel to other cities and countries I haven't gone before. Hence, it was very important for me to have a job while studying. Of course, if I asked my parents, they would give me anything, but I didn't want to do that as I wanted to be independent and find a job on my own.

I use the extra income from the job to do many different things. To start with, I use the income to visit new places in the country. I go out with friends on the weekends and sometimes pay the bills myself. As a medical student, I do not get much time to enjoy, so I make sure to make the most of my free time. Most importantly, I want to save for the future as it will help me in any emergencies, such as a major health expense that's not covered by insurance.

What are your hopes in life after graduation?

After graduation, I want to work in my home country as a General Practitioner for a few years. I would ideally work in a large hospital, but I might choose to work in a clinic as well. After 1 or 2 years of practicing, I then want to go abroad, hopefully to the UK, and start my postgraduate training in a recognized hospital in order to specialize in Neurosurgery. The main reason I want to become a Neurosurgeon is because there are only a few doctors in my country specialized in neurosurgery.

As a neurosurgeon, my job will involve the diagnosis and surgical treatment of patients with neurologic diseases. These include diseases of the brain, spinal cord, and nerves. Then, when I have enough knowledge and experience, I plan on training new residents and interns in the hospital.

In the future, I would like to expand my freelancing career. In addition to writing medical content and articles, I want to provide online consultations too, which I believe will save a lot of time for those who are too busy to visit a hospital. Plus, working with people in different parts of the world will give me considerable experience.

A word of wisdom for students trying to get their first job

I have a few pieces of advice for you if you choose to freelance while studying. But first, you must know that freelancing will be extremely difficult in the beginning. It won't be easy to get your first job because clients won't hire you due to your lack of experience. Also, the competition on freelancing platforms is huge and many people give up after a few months of trying.

But the real question is, how far are you willing to go? If you are determined to make your career a success, then you can and you will. That should be your mindset. Keep applying to jobs until you receive an invitation. Trust me, it's just a matter of time until you receive an offer.

However, do not apply to jobs that don't match your skills. This is one of the worst mistakes that new freelancers make. They take jobs that they can't do and, in the end, deliver something that neither of them, nor their client, is satisfied with. This results in them getting bad feedback and decreasing their chances of getting another job.

If there's a job that you are 100% confident about, go for it even if the budget is low. Remember that your first job might not be your 'dream job'. But if you do it well, you will get a great review which will really help you in the future.

Be professional! The way you communicate with your client matters a lot. If they ask for a video call for the interview, do not show up in your pajamas. Yes, you are working from home, but you should dress professionally as it will create a positive impression about you in the client's mind.

Finally, enjoy your job! Your first job can be very rewarding, and you must make the most out of it. I wish you all the best!

Being true to yourself

Jane Wanja - Kenya

Why did you choose your current university course?

Since my second year in high school, I knew I always wanted to do something technical. I have always been one to take on new challenges avidly. I realized earlier on that doing the same thing time and again can be plodding. In my culture, being a girl, the presupposition was that I would either become a doctor or a lawyer, the 'girls' careers as they are termed. However, I always relished the technical subjects, with physics and mathematics being my favorite.

I cannot emphasize enough how much I specifically disliked Biology. I remember my parent's tenacity in wanting me to become the first family doctor of which they ingeniously sounded happy about. The thought of letting them down made my stomach churn and in turn, I became an addled 14-year-old.

Luckily for me, my high school had a program whereby the alumni would have an entire day to hold meetings and talks with the current students about their careers, experiences, salaries, requirements and the different options that were available in the specific fields. I had never heard of architecture before, as it is one of the career paths that was described as heretic. It was until this lady said she was an architect.

It immediately caught my attention, and I became antsy to know all the details of becoming one. She talked about the technicalities and creative aspects of the course, and I knew right there and then that it was what I wanted to do. My father's career background is in business and so he ended up convincing me to now shift to a Bachelor of Commerce, after I had been admitted to a school off-shore for a Bachelor's Degree in Architecture.

His argument was that he needed someone to run the company due to his impending retirement. I changed my degree and got admitted to the top university for BCom. Since the course didn't start until a year later, I decided to intern at his office to envisage the world of commerce. Dare I say, I became depressed within the first three weeks of working there. Now, that is not to say that the world is dreary, it is just how I operate as an individual. I then came to terms that it wasn't working for me, so I talked with my father, and he agreed to let me revert to architecture but in a different school that was closer.

It has been three and a half years now. I'm about to graduate and even though sometimes it gets strenuous and demanding, I enjoy most of it, including the sleepless nights.

What was your first job while you were studying?

After two years of joining campus, I wanted to start running my own side venture to earn some extra income. I was totally dependent on my parents for my fees, rent and subsistence. I had several ideas but the capital was unfeasible. Since I wasn't able to raise that money, I started looking for online jobs that require no capital investment. I went through loads of online videos on how to work online with just a laptop and a stable internet connection, and there was a synonymous discounting on how hard it was to land and earn from these jobs.

I always thought that maybe, as long as one had the skills, jobs would be easy to find. That was not the case. It was not until recently that I found a video that mentioned a popular online freelancing website that I decided to give it a go. There was no registration fee and you got to send in proposals for the kind of jobs that you are suited for.

My expectation was a bit delirious seeing all the job listings being made every minute on this application. However, I came to a quick realization that in order to land your first job, you have to send several proposals to different clients, most of which will be rejected.

The earlier you come to that "aha!" moment of realizing that there is always a more proficient person in that field than you are, the earlier the load's turndown becomes a bit tolerable. The secret is to be resilient and consistent.

So, the question about my first job? I finally landed one and working on my experience as a new member may help someone in the same position as I am to not give up. There is hope so keep at it.

How important is having a job for you while you are studying?

There are two major reasons why I remain unrelenting on getting extra income. The first one might be similar to many people, current fortuitous events in the world. The pandemic has affected most businesses, including my father's, and my fees are quite significant. My intention is to use my expertise so that I can chip in on paying for my pocket money, instead of being completely dependent on him.

Being 21-years of age, I am privy to the fluctuant state of businesses. Therefore, being able to provide for myself when my parents are unable to intervene is crucial.

The other reason is to build myself up to financial freedom. As I see it, becoming independent, understanding how money works, and how to make money work for me is vitally important.

I have been on a journey to financial literacy; the things that they don't teach you in schools such as, financial management, tax payment, savings, and investments. This information is imperative when building a life that you want for yourself. I have younger siblings who, in the future, will depend on me for responsibilities such as paying for their school fees.

Also, as a woman, financial independence is crucial because I get to make my own decisions regarding money without relying on someone else.

What are your hopes in life after graduation?

After my graduation from my fourth year, the contingency is to join a university overseas to do my master's degree, preferably in Australia. On completion, I hope to come back to my country where I'll start my career as an architect. The prerequisite however, following graduation from my sixth year, is to work under a registered architect for about two years after which I will sit a national regulatory exam before becoming certified as a practicing architect. On passing, one can proceed to set up their personal practice where you are able to specialize in whatever niche you would like, be it residential, commercial, renovations, interior design among others.

The prospects are still unclear for me, but I tend to lean more towards the urban planning sector. The idea is to provide quality housing for every social class in urban areas that are sustainable and affordable using innovativeness and reduction of regulatory barriers. Later on in my career, I hope to join policy makers in the field since these are the people who have the mandate to shape how the industry works. Being a part of them would then mean providing ingenious insights and ideas to promote the course to a more sustainable and greener built environment.

A word of wisdom for students trying to get their first job

Finally, my advice is simple - keep at it. These three words have seen me through some of the most grievous of times. Relatively, for our generation, we have grown up in a time of the internet where everything is just a click away, which is usually a good thing. On the flip side however, it means that we have become accustomed to instant gratification, which is not necessarily what happens in real life.

For those of you who are looking for jobs, it may take a while to land one. These days, networking is requisite. It's the world that we live in. My father keeps telling me that the main reason you are at university is to create networks. The same people you sit with at the café eating meals together, regardless of the course they are taking, are the same people you are going to work with once you leave university.

Whether you are soft-spoken or an outgoing person, this is a skill that you should master. Endeavor to create a network of people that may help you in the future when you are stuck with your taxes and need someone to audit them for you.

Also, understand the difference between acquaintances and friends. Great friends are people that will mention your name in a boardroom when a company is looking for a person of your skillset, as you strive to be the same for your friends.

Dreams of working abroad

Amr Ehab - Egypt

Why did you choose your current university course?

I studied in an English language school where I was an average student. My grades weren't the highest, but I enjoyed it. After I graduated from school, I made the decision to join the medical field. I chose physiotherapy because physiotherapists make more money than other medical professions here in Egypt and are more likely to get a job. As physiotherapists are few in numbers, it's also easier for them to work abroad. Plus, it turns out that physiotherapy is not just about that; as my professor always says "Medicine adds days to life, while physiotherapy adds life to days"

My perspective about this career changed after I saw kids who suffer from Poliomyelitis and brain atrophy. Those kids weren't able to move, eat or play properly as normal kids, but after finishing therapy, they became normal as if they weren't even sick before, which changed their whole life. I have also seen people suffer from back pain due to disorders in their spinal cord which require surgery that can easily be treated with physiotherapy.

What was your first job while you were studying?

I got my first job after my first semester in university. As I grew up, my needs got more expensive, I had to move to another city where my university is, and now I have to pay for food, pay rent and bills. My father only helped me during the first semester. Then my parents got divorced and my father decided that he wouldn't help me anymore because I chose to live with my mother.

So, I had to find a job and luckily it wasn't hard. My aunt is a pharmacist. She helped me find a job at her friend's pharmacy and taught me everything I needed to know to work there. I also had a month of training with someone who worked there for a while. It was an easy job. All I had to do was read the doctor's prescription and get the medicine off the shelf; we are not allowed to prescribe medicine or doses, only the pharmacist can, which made it easier for me.

However, there were two things that I didn't like about this job. The first one was that it was sometimes boring; sometimes, I would stay for hours just sitting there with nothing to do because there were no clients. The other is that the doctor's writing is sometimes completely unreadable.

How important is having a job for you while you are studying?

It's very important to have a job while you are studying. Most students feel like having a job might distract them from studying, but I say it's possible to do both work and study. It might become hard to keep up during exams. I always take holiday during my final exams, so I can focus more on studying.

Having a job helps you in a lot of ways. A job can help you avoid being in debt. I myself use this money very wisely, spending most of it on basics such as rent, bills, food and clothes, and keeping the rest of it until needed. For instance, I might need to buy a new phone, upgrade my laptop, or maybe help my mother with her payments in case she needs help.

Of course, the best thing about this is not having to ask for money every time I want to buy something. This extra money can be very useful, and if your parents are helping to pay your living costs, you end up having so much extra money that you can save for your future.

What are your hopes in life after graduation?

After graduation, I want to work with what I learned as a physiotherapist. The first thing I'm going to do is to apply for a DPT (Doctorate of Physical Therapy), which will give me more experience and training. It will also become handy in case I want to work abroad, as most countries now require physiotherapists to have a DPT before they can work.

I hope I get a chance to work in another country. Luckily, in my country, physiotherapists are more likely to get a job abroad than others in the medical field, but there is something else that I also want to achieve one day...

I also have always wanted to own a computer store, as I'm really passionate about technology. This has been my dream since I was a kid. I hope that I can achieve it one day, and I hope all this can help me to live as I always wanted; I always dreamed of having a nice big house and a fancy electric car.

A word of wisdom for students trying to get their first job

My advice to other students is to get started. It doesn't matter how much experience you have, it can always be increased. if you don't have any experience, you can still learn from scratch. For example, I applied to a course to learn how to make and edit websites, so I have new job opportunities.

There is also freelancing which gives a lot of opportunities for people to find jobs online. Once, I heard a motivational speaker say "You don't have to be great to start, but you have to start to be great", which was the best advice I ever heard. So basically, all you have to do is to get started. It doesn't matter if it takes you a month or two to learn a new thing that you can work with, just start it and be patient.

Imagine the free life that you will have; no more asking for money or being in debt. It might require effort to keep up with studying and working at the same time, but I personally think that it's totally worth it. If you don't agree with me, you can try it for a month or two to see if it fits in your life or not, then make a decision.

Afterword

There was a time before my life was consumed by looking after my family, and running my business, that I would take some time to visit old workplaces and visit people who have made a significant difference in my life. They were always happy to welcome me regardless of whether they had clients waiting or not.

I would tell them about my ideas, about the things that have happened between my times of visits. I would call up an old employer every now and again, but now as a colleague rather than an employee. I also loved to visit my old high school and tell them about the things that have happened, until all my old teachers left! Hopefully this wasn't because of me.

The truth is this, and I can't speak for anyone else, I love hearing about people who do well. Each and every one of the names in this book are special to me. So, what are my hopes and dreams for these students after they graduate? That one day their experiences encourage many others, and that one day many years in the future, I will see one of these names become a successful person in the global community.

Although I believe it would be wishful thinking on my part, I would love an opportunity in years from now to meet these new leaders of tomorrow in person for a coffee and a chat. A chat about struggles, experiences and hopes for the future. Nothing really changes, does it?

Be encouraged by these stories and do the best you can so you can also be an inspiration to others around you.

Get Your First Job as a University Student

If you enjoyed this book you can visit our website to read many more stories.

arthurlee.com.au

More Titles to come!

www.ingramcontent.com/pod-product-compliance
Lightning Source LLC
Chambersburg PA
CBHW052338220526
45472CB00001B/482